Love Struck!

Love Poems:
Five Centuries of Romantic Verse

Selected by
George Nichols

THE CLAPTON PRESS
LONDON E5

Published by:

The Clapton Press Limited
38 Thistlewaite Road
London E5 0QQ

ISBN-13:978-1-9996543-3-7

For Kathryn

Love Struck!

THE CLAPTON PRESS
LONDON E5

CONTENTS   Page:

CONTENTS   Page:

CONTENTS   Page:

Alfred Austin
(1835-1913)

Love's Trinity

Soul, heart, and body, we thus singly name,
Are not in love divisible and distinct,
But each with each inseparably linked.
One is not honour, and the other shame,
But burn as closely fused as fuel, heat, and flame.

They do not love who give the body and keep
The heart ungiven; nor they who yield the soul,
And guard the body. Love doth give the whole;
Its range being high as heaven, as ocean deep,
Wide as the realms of air or planet's curving sweep.

Lord Alfred Douglas

(1870-1945)

Two loves

I dreamed I stood upon a little hill,
And at my feet there lay a ground, that seemed
Like a waste garden, flowering at its will
With buds and blossoms. There were pools that
  dreamed
Black and unruffled; there were white lilies
A few, and crocuses, and violets
Purple or pale, snake-like fritillaries
Scarce seen for the rank grass, and through green
  nets
Blue eyes of shy peryenche winked in the sun.
And there were curious flowers, before unknown,
Flowers that were stained with moonlight, or with
  shades
Of Nature's willful moods; and here a one
That had drunk in the transitory tone
Of one brief moment in a sunset; blades
Of grass that in an hundred springs had been
Slowly but exquisitely nurtured by the stars,
And watered with the scented dew long cupped
In lilies, that for rays of sun had seen
Only God's glory, for never a sunrise mars
The luminous air of Heaven. Beyond, abrupt,
A grey stone wall o'ergrown with velvet moss
Uprose; and gazing I stood long, all mazed
To see a place so strange, so sweet, so fair.
And as I stood and marvelled, lo! across
The garden came a youth; one hand he raised

Lord Alfred Douglas
(1870-1945)

[...]

To shield him from the sun, his wind-tossed hair
Was twined with flowers, and in his hand he bore
A purple bunch of bursting grapes, his eyes
Were clear as crystal, naked all was he,
White as the snow on pathless mountains frore,
Red were his lips as red wine-spilith that dyes
A marble floor, his brow chalcedony.
And he came near me, with his lips uncurled
And kind, and caught my hand and kissed my
  mouth,
And gave me grapes to eat, and said, "Sweet friend,
Come I will show thee shadows of the world
And images of life. See from the South
Comes the pale pageant that hath never an end."
And lo! within the garden of my dream
I saw two walking on a shining plain
Of golden light. The one did joyous seem
And fair and blooming, and a sweet refrain
Came from his lips; he sang of pretty maids
And joyous love of comely girl and boy,
His eyes were bright, and 'mid the dancing blades
Of golden grass his feet did trip for joy;
And in his hand he held an ivory lute
With strings of gold that were as maidens' hair,
And sang with voice as tuneful as a flute,
And round his neck three chains of roses were.
But he that was his comrade walked aside;

Lord Alfred Douglas
(1870-1945)

[...]

He was full sad and sweet, and his large eyes
Were strange with wondrous brightness, staring
  wide
With gazing; and he sighed with many sighs
That moved me, and his cheeks were wan and white
Like pallid lilies, and his lips were red
Like poppies, and his hands he clenched tight,
And yet again unclenched, and his head
Was wreathed with moon-flowers pale as lips of
  death.
A purple robe he wore, o'erwrought in gold
With the device of a great snake, whose breath
Was fiery flame: which when I did behold
I fell-aweeping, and I cried, "Sweet youth,
Tell me why, sad and sighing, thou dost rove
These pleasant realms? I pray thee speak me sooth
What is thy name?" He said, "My name is Love."
Then straight the first did turn himself to me
And cried, "He lieth, for his name is Shame,
But I am Love, and I was wont to be
Alone in this fair garden, till he came
Unasked by night; I am true Love, I fill
The hearts of boy and girl with mutual flame."
Then sighing, said the other, "Have thy will,
I am the love that dare not speak its name."

Alfred Lord Tennyson
(1809-1892)

Now Sleeps the Crimson Petal

Now sleeps the crimson petal, now the white;
Nor waves the cypress in the palace walk;
Nor winks the gold fin in the porphyry font:
The fire-fly wakens; waken thou with me.

Now droops the milk-white peacock like a ghost,
And like a ghost she glimmers on to me.

Now lies the Earth all Danaë to the stars,
And all thy heart lies open unto me.

Now slides the silent meteor on, and leaves
A shining furrow, as thy thoughts in me.

Now folds the lily all her sweetness up,
And slips into the bosom of the lake:
So fold thyself, my dearest, thou, and slip
Into my bosom and be lost in me.

Alfred Lord Tennyson
(1809-1892)

O That 'twere Possible

O that 'twere possible
After long grief and pain
To find the arms of my true love
Round me once again!
A shadow flits before me,
Not thou, but like to thee:
Ah, Christ! That it were possible
For one short hour to see
The souls we loved, that they might tell us
What and where they be!

Alfred Lord Tennyson
(1809-1892)

The Beggar Maid

Her arms across her breast she laid,
She was more fair than words can say:
Bare-footed came the beggar maid
Before the king Cophetua.
In robe and crown the king stept down,
To meet and greet her on her way;
"It is no wonder," said the lords,
"She is more beautiful than day".

As shines the moon in clouded skies,
She in her poor attire was seen:
One praised her ancles, one her eyes,
One her dark hair and lovesome mien:
So sweet a face, such angel grace,
In all that land had never been:
Cophetua sware a royal oath:
"This beggar maid shall be my queen!"

Amy Lowell
(1824-1925)

The Bungler

You glow in my heart
Like the flames of uncounted candles.
But when I go to warm my hands,
My clumsiness overturns the light,
And then I stumble
Against the tables and chairs.

Amy Lowell
(1824-1925)

The Taxi

When I go away from you
The world beats dead
Like a slackened drum.
I call out for you against the jutted stars
And shout into the ridges of the wind.
Streets coming fast,
One after the other,
Wedge you away from me,
And the lamps of the city prick my eyes
So that I can no longer see your face.
Why should I leave you,
To wound myself upon the sharp edges of the
    night?

Amy Lowell
(1874-1925)

Madonna of the Evening Flowers

All day long I have been working
Now I am tired.
I call: "Where are you?"
But there is only the oak tree rustling in the
  wind.
The house is very quiet,
The sun shines in on your books,
On your scissors and thimble just put down,
But you are not there.
Suddenly I am lonely:
Where are you?
I go about searching.
Then I see you,
Standing under a spire of pale blue larkspur,
With a basket of roses on your arm.
You are cool, like silver,
And you smile.
I think the Canterbury bells are playing little
    tunes,
You tell me that the peonies need spraying,
That the columbines have overrun all bounds,
That the pyrus japonica should be cut back and
  rounded.
You tell me these things.
But I look at you, heart of silver,
White heart-flame of polished silver,
Burning beneath the blue steeples of the
  larkspur,
And I long to kneel instantly at your feet,
While all about us peal the loud, sweet
Te Deums of the Canterbury bells.

Andrew Marvell
(1621-1678)

The Fair Singer

To make a final conquest of all me,
Love did compose so sweet an enemy,
In whom both beauties to my death agree,
Joining themselves in fatal harmony;
That while she with her eyes my heart does bind,
She with her voice might captivate my mind.

I could have fled from one but singly fair,
My disentangled soul itself might save,
Breaking the curled trammels of her hair.
But how should I avoid to be her slave,
Whose subtle art invisibly can wreath
My fetters of the very air I breathe?

It had been easy fighting in some plain,
Where victory might hang in equal choice,
But all resistance against her is vain,
Who has the advantage both of eyes and voice,
And all my forces needs must be undone,
She having gained both the wind and sun.

Andrew Marvell
(1621-1678)

To His Coy Mistress

Had we but world enough, and time,
This coyness, lady, were no crime.
We would sit down, and think which way
To walk, and pass our long love's day.
Thou by the Indian Ganges' side
Shouldst rubies find; I by the tide
Of Humber would complain. I would
Love you ten years before the flood,
And you should, if you please, refuse
Till the conversion of the Jews.
My vegetable love would grow
Vaster than empires, and more slow;
An hundred years should go to praise
Thine eyes, and on thy forehead gaze;
Two hundred to adore each breast,
But thirty thousand to the rest;
An age at least to every part,
And the last age should show your heart.
For, lady, you deserve this state,
Nor would I love at lower rate.

But at my back I always hear
Time's winged chariot hurrying near:
And yonder all before us lie
Deserts of vast eternity.
Thy beauty shall no more be found;
Nor, in thy marble vaults, shall sound

Andrew Marvell
(1621-1678)

[...]

My echoing song; then worms shall try
That long-preserved virginity,
And your quaint honour turn to dust,
And into ashes all my lust:
The grave's a fine and private place,
But none, I think, do there embrace.
Now therefore, while the youthful hue
Sits on thy skin like morning dew,
And while thy willing soul transpires
At every pore with instant fires,
Now let us sport us while we may,
And now, like amorous birds of prey,
Rather at once our time devour
Than languish in his slow-chapped power.
Let us roll all our strength, and all
Our sweetness, up into one ball,
And tear our pleasure with rough strife
Through the iron gates of life:
Thus, though we cannot make our sun
Stand still, yet we will make him run.

Anne Bradstreet
(1612-1672)

To My Dear and Loving Husband

If ever two were one, then surely we.
If ever man were loved by wife, then thee;
If ever wife was happy in a man,
Compare with me ye women if you can.
I prize thy love more than whole mines of gold,
Or all the riches that the East doth hold.
My love is such that rivers cannot quench,
Nor ought but love from thee give recompense.
Thy love is such I can no way repay;
The heavens reward thee manifold, I pray.
Then while we live, in love let's so persever,
That when we live no more we may live ever.

Anon
before 1530

Western Wind

Western wind, when wilt thou blow,
The small rain down can rain.
Christ, if my love were in my arms,
And I in my bed again.

Aphra Behn
(1640-1689)

A Thousand Martyrs I Have Made

A thousand martyrs I have made,
All sacrificed to my desire;
A thousand beauties have betrayed,
That languish in resistless fire.
The untamed heart to hand I brought,
And fixed the wild and wandering thought.

I never vowed nor sighed in vain
But both, though false, were well received.
The fair are pleased to give us pain,
And what they wish is soon believed.
And though I talked of wounds and smart,
Love's pleasures only touched my heart.

Alone the glory and the spoil
I always laughing bore away;
The triumphs, without pain or toil,
Without the hell, the heaven of joy.
And while I thus at random rove
Despise the fools that whine for love.

Aphra Behn
(1640-1689)

The Willing Mistriss

Amyntas led me to a grove,
Where all the trees did shade us;
The sun itself, though it had strove,
It could not have betrayed us:
The place secured from human eyes,
No other fear allows,
But when the winds that gently rise,
Do kiss the yielding boughs.

Down there we sat upon the moss,
And did begin to play
A thousand amorous tricks, to pass
The heat of all the day.
A many kisses he did give:
And I returned the same
Which made me willing to receive
That which I dare not name.
His charming eyes no aid required
To tell their softening tale;
On her that was already fired,
'Twas easy to prevail.
He did but kiss and clasp me round,
Whilst those his thoughts expressed:
And layed me gently on the ground:
Ah, who can guess the rest?

Ben Johnson
(1572-1637)

Song to Celia

Drink to me only with thine eyes,
   And I will pledge with mine;
Or leave a kiss but in the cup,
   And I'll not look for wine.
The thirst that from the soul doth rise
   Doth ask a drink divine;
But might I of Jove's nectar sup,
   I would not change for thine.

I sent thee late a rosy wreath,
   Not so much honouring thee
As giving it a hope, that there
   It could not withered be.
But thou thereon didst only breathe,
   And sent'st it back to me

Since when it grows, and smells, I swear,
   Not of itself, but thee.

Christina Rossetti
(1830-1894)

A Birthday

My heart is like a singing bird
Whose nest is in a watered shoot;
My heart is like an apple-tree
Whose boughs are bent with thick-set fruit;
My heart is like a rainbow shell
That paddles in a halcyon sea;
My heart is gladder than all these
Because my love is come to me.

Raise me a daïs of silk and down;
Hang it with vair and purple dyes;
Carve it in doves and pomegranates,
And peacocks with a hundred eyes;
Work it in gold and silver grapes,
In leaves and silver fleurs-de-lys;
Because the birthday of my life
Is come, my love is come to me.

Christina Rossetti
(1830-1894)

I Loved You First

Poca favilla gran fiamma seconda. – Dante

Ogni altra cosa, ogni pensier va fore,
E sol ivi con voi rimansi amore. – Petrarca

I loved you first: but afterwards your love
Outsoaring mine, sang such a loftier song
As drowned the friendly cooings of my dove.
Which owes the other most? my love was long,
And yours one moment seemed to wax more
    strong;
I loved and guessed at you, you construed me
And loved me for what might or might not be–
Nay, weights and measures do us both a wrong.
For verily love knows not "mine" or "thine;"
With separate "I" and "thou" free love has done,
For one is both and both are one in love:
Rich love knows nought of "thine that is not mine;"
Both have the strength and both the length thereof,
Both of us, of the love which makes us one.

Christina Rossetti
(1830-1894)

Song

When I am dead, my dearest,
Sing no sad songs for me;
Plant thou no roses at my head,
Nor shady cypress tree:
Be the green grass above me
With showers and dewdrops wet:
And if thou wilt, remember,
And if thou wilt, forget.

I shall not see the shadows,
I shall not feel the rain;
I shall not hear the nightingale
Sing on as if in pain:
And dreaming through the twilight
That doth not rise nor set,
Haply I may remember,
And haply may forget.

Christopher Marlowe
(1564-1593)

Dr Faustus, Act V, Scene 1

Was this the face that launched a thousand ships,
And burnt the topless towers of Ilium—
Sweet Helen, make me immortal with a kiss.—
Her lips suck forth my soul: see, where it flies!—
Come, Helen, come, give me my soul again.
Here will I dwell, for heaven is in these lips,
And all is dross that is not Helena.
I will be Paris, and for love of thee,
Instead of Troy, shall Wertenberg be sacked;
And I will combat with weak Menelaus,
And wear thy colours on my plumed crest;
Yea, I will wound Achilles in the heel,
And then return to Helen for a kiss.
O, thou art fairer than the evening air
Clad in the beauty of a thousand stars;
Brighter art thou than flaming Jupiter
When he appeared to hapless Semele;
More lovely than the monarch of the sky
In wanton Arethus's azured arms;
And none but thou shalt be my paramour!

Christopher Marlowe
(1564-1593)

It Lies Not In Our Power

It lies not in our power to love or hate,
For will in us is overruled by fate.
When two are stripped, long ere the course begin,
We wish that one should love, the other win;
And one especially do we affect
Of two gold ingots, like in each respect:
The reason no man knows; let it suffice
What we behold is censured by our eyes.
Where both deliberate, the love is slight:
Who ever loved, that loved not at first sight?

Christopher Marlowe
(1564-1593)

The Passionate Shepherd to His Love

Come live with me and be my love,
And we will all the pleasures prove,
That valleys, groves, hills, and fields,
Woods, or steepy mountain yields.

And we will sit upon the rocks,
Seeing the shepherds feed their flocks,
By shallow rivers to whose falls
Melodious birds sing madrigals.

And I will make thee beds of roses
And a thousand fragrant posies,
A cap of flowers, and a kirtle
Embroidered all with leaves of myrtle;

A gown made of the finest wool
Which from our pretty lambs we pull;
Fair lined slippers for the cold,
With buckles of the purest gold;

A belt of straw and Ivy buds,
With coral clasps and amber studs:
And if these pleasures may thee move,
Come live with me, and be my love.

The shepherds' swains shall dance and sing
For thy delight each May-morning:
If these delights thy mind may move,
Then live with me, and be my love.

Sir Walter Raleigh
(1552-1618)

Her Reply

If all the world and love were young,
And truth in every shepherd's tongue,
These pretty pleasures might me move
To live with thee and be thy love.

But time drives flocks from field to fold;
When rivers rage and rocks grow cold;
And Philomel becometh dumb;
The rest complains of cares to come.

The flowers do fade, and wanton fields
To wayward winter reckoning yields:
A honey tongue, a heart of gall,
Is fancy's spring, but sorrow's fall.

Thy gowns, thy shoes, thy beds of roses,
Thy cap, thy kirtle, and thy posies,
Soon break, soon wither—soon forgotten,
In folly ripe, in reason rotten.

Thy belt of straw and ivy-buds,
Thy coral clasps and amber studs—
All these in me no means can move
To come to thee and be thy love.

But could youth last, and love still breed,
Had joys no date, nor age no need,
Then these delights my mind might move
To live with thee and be thy love.

Dante Gabriel Rossetti
(1828-1882)

Sudden Light

I have been here before,
But when or how I cannot tell:
I know the grass beyond the door,
The sweet keen smell,
The sighing sound, the lights around the shore.

You have been mine before—
How long ago I may not know:
But just when at that swallow's soar
Your neck turned so,
Some veil did fall—I knew it all of yore.

Has this been thus before?
And shall not thus time's eddying flight
Still with our lives our love restore
In death's despite,
And day and night yield one delight once more?

David Herbert Lawrence
(1885-1930)

On the Balcony

In front of the sombre mountains,
a faint, lost ribbon of rainbow;
And between us and it, the thunder;
And down below in the green wheat,
   the labourers
Stand like dark stumps, still in the green wheat.

You are near to me,
and your naked feet in their sandals,
And through the scent of the balcony's naked
   timber
I distinguish the scent of your hair: so now the
   limber
Lightning falls from heaven.

Adown the pale-green glacier river floats
A dark boat through the gloom—and whither?
The thunder roars. But still we have each other!
The naked lightnings in the heavens dither
And disappear—what have we but each other?
The boat has gone.

Edgar Allan Poe
(1809-1849)

Annabel Lee

It was many and many a year ago,
  In a kingdom by the sea,
That a maiden there lived whom you may know
  By the name of Annabel Lee;
And this maiden she lived with no other thought
  Than to love and be loved by me.

I was a child and *she* was a child,
  In this kingdom by the sea,
But we loved with a love that was more than love—
  I and my Annabel Lee—
With a love that the wingèd seraphs of Heaven
  Coveted her and me.

And this was the reason that, long ago,
  In this kingdom by the sea,
A wind blew out of a cloud, chilling
  My beautiful Annabel Lee;
So that her highborn kinsmen came
  And bore her away from me,
To shut her up in a sepulchre
  In this kingdom by the sea.

The angels, not half so happy in Heaven,
  Went envying her and me—
Yes!—that was the reason (as all men know,
  In this kingdom by the sea)
That the wind came out of the cloud by night,
  Chilling and killing my Annabel Lee.

Edgar Allan Poe
(1809-1849)

[...]

But our love it was stronger by far than the love
  Of those who were older than we—
  Of many far wiser than we—
And neither the angels in Heaven above
  Nor the demons down under the sea
Can ever dissever my soul from the soul
  Of the beautiful Annabel Lee;

For the moon never beams, without bringing me
    dreams
  Of the beautiful Annabel Lee;
And the stars never rise, but I feel the bright eyes
  Of the beautiful Annabel Lee;
And so, all the night-tide, I lie down by the side
  Of my darling—my darling—my life and my bride,
  In her sepulchre there by the sea—
  In her tomb by the sounding sea.

Edgar Allan Poe

(1809-1849)

Eulalie

I dwelt alone
In a world of moan,
And my soul was a stagnant tide,
Till the fair and gentle Eulalie became my blushing
bride–
Till the yellow-haired young Eulalie became my
smiling bride.

Ah, less–less bright
The stars of the night
Than the eyes of the radiant girl!
That the vapor can make
With the moon-tints of purple and pearl,
Can vie with the modest Eulalie's most unregarded
curl–

Can compare with the bright-eyed Eulalie's most
humble and careless curl.
Now doubt–now pain
Come never again,
For her soul gives me sigh for sigh,
And all day long
Shines, bright and strong,
Astarte within the sky,
While ever to her dear Eulalie upturns her matron
eye–
While ever to her young Eulalie upturns her violet
eye.

Edgar Allan Poe
(1809-1849)

A Dream Within a Dream

Take this kiss upon the brow!
And, in parting from you now,
Thus much let me avow-
You are not wrong, who deem
That my days have been a dream;
Yet, if hope has flown away
In a night, or in a day,
In a vision, or in none,
Is it, therefore, the less gone?
All that we see or seem
Is but a dream within a dream.

I stand amid the roar
Of a surf-tormented shore,
And I hold within my hand
Grains of golden sand-
How few! yet how they creep
Through my fingers to the deep,
While I weep- while I weep!
O God! can I not grasp
Them with a tighter clasp?
O God! can I not save
One from the pitiless wave?
Is all that we see or seem
But a dream within a dream?

Edmund Spenser
(1552-1599)

My Love is Like to Ice, and I to Fire

My love is like to ice, and I to fire:
How come it then that this her cold is so great,
Is not dissolved through my so hot desire,
But harder grows the more I her entreat?
Or how comes it that my exceeding heat
Is not allayed by her heart-frozen cold,
But that I burn much more in boiling sweat,
And feel my flames augmented manifold?
What more miraculous thing may be told,
That fire, which is congealed with senseless cold,
Should kindle fire by wonderful device?
Such is the power of love in gentle mind,
That it can alter all the course of kind.

Edmund Spenser
(1552-1599)

Amoretti LXXV

One day I wrote her name upon the strand,
But came the waves and washed it away;
Again I wrote it with a second hand,
But came the tide, and made my pains his prey.
"Vain man," said she, "that dost in vain assay,
A mortal thing so to immortalize;
For I myself shall like to this decay,
And eke my name be wiped out likewise."
"Not so," (quod I) "let baser things devise
To die in dust, but you shall live by fame:
My verse your vertues write your glorious name:
Where whenas death shall all the world subdue,
Our love shall live, and later life renew."

Edmund Waller
(1606-1674)

On a Girdle

That which her slender waist confined,
Shall now my joyful temples bind;
No monarch but would give his crown,
His arms might do what this has done.

It was my heaven's extremest sphere,
The pale which held that lovely deer,
My joy, my grief, my hope, my love,
Did all within this circle move.

A narrow compass, and yet there
Dwelt all that's good, and all that's fair;
Give me but what this ribband bound,
Take all the rest the sun goes round.

Edmund Waller
(1606-1674)

Go, Lovely Rose

Go, lovely Rose,—
Tell her that wastes her time and me,
That now she knows,
When I resemble her to thee,
How sweet and fair she seems to be.

Tell her that's young,
And shuns to have her graces spied,
That hadst thou sprung
In deserts where no men abide,
Thou must have uncommended died.

Small is the worth
Of beauty from the light retired:
Bid her come forth,
Suffer herself to be desired,
And not blush so to be admired.

Then die—that she
The common fate of all things rare
May read in thee;
How small a part of time they share
That are so wondrous sweet and fair!

Edward Lear
(1812-1888)

The Owl and the Pussy-Cat

The Owl and the Pussy-cat went to sea
  In a beautiful pea-green boat,
They took some honey, and plenty of money,
  Wrapped up in a five-pound note.
The Owl looked up to the stars above,
  And sang to a small guitar,
"O lovely Pussy! O Pussy, my love,
  What a beautiful Pussy you are,
     You are,
     You are!
What a beautiful Pussy you are!"

Pussy said to the Owl, "You elegant fowl!
  How charmingly sweet you sing!
O let us be married! too long we have tarried:
  But what shall we do for a ring?"
They sailed away, for a year and a day,
  To the land where the Bong-Tree grows
And there in a wood a Piggy-wig stood
  With a ring at the end of his nose,
     His nose,
     His nose,
  With a ring at the end of his nose.

Edward Lear
(1812-1888)

[...]

"Dear Pig, are you willing to sell for one shilling
   Your ring?" Said the Piggy, "I will."
So they took it away, and were married next day
   By the Turkey who lives on the hill.
They dined on mince, and slices of quince,
   Which they ate with a runcible spoon;
And hand in hand, on the edge of the sand,
   They danced by the light of the moon,
         The moon,
         The moon,
They danced by the light of the moon.

Edward Thomas
(1878-1897)

Like The Touch of Rain She Was

Like the touch of rain she was
On a man's flesh and hair and eyes
When the joy of walking thus
Has taken him by surprise:

With the love of the storm he burns,
He sings, he laughs, well I know how,
But forgets when he returns
As I shall not forget her "Go now".

Those two words shut a door
Between me and the blessed rain
That was never shut before
And will not open again.

Edward Thomas
(1878-1897)

The Sorrow of True Love

The sorrow of true love is a great sorrow
And true love parting blackens a bright morrow:
Yet almost they equal joys, since their despair
Is but hope blinded by its tears, and clear
Above the storm the heavens wait to be seen.
But greater sorrow from less love has been
That can mistake lack of despair for hope
And knows not tempest and the perfect scope
Of summer, but a frozen drizzle perpetual
Of drops that from remorse and pity fall
And cannot ever shine in the sun or thaw,
Removed eternally from the sun's law.

Elizabeth Barrett Browning
(1806-1861)

I Love You Not Only
For What You Are

I love you not only for what you are
but for what I am when I am with you.
I love you not only for what you have made of
  yourself
but for what you are making of me.
I love you for the part of me that you bring out.

Elizabeth Barrett Browning
(1806-1861)

Sonnet XVIII

How do I love thee? Let me count the ways.
I love thee to the depth and breadth and height
My soul can reach, when feeling out of sight
For the ends of being and ideal grace.
I love thee freely, as men strive for right.
I love thee purely, as they turn from praise.
I love thee with the passion put to use
In my old griefs, and with my childhood's faith.
I love thee with a love I seemed to lose
With my lost saints. I love thee with the breath,
Smiles, tears, of all my life; and, if God choose,
I shall but love thee better after death.

Elizabeth Barrett Browning
(1806-1861)

Love

We cannot live, except thus mutually
We alternate, aware or unaware,
The reflex act of life: and when we bear
Our virtue onward most impulsively,
Most full of invocation, and to be
Most instantly compellant, certes, there
We live most life, whoever breathes most air
And counts his dying years by sun and sea.
But when a soul, by choice and conscience, doth
Throw out her full force on another soul,
The conscience and the concentration both
Make mere life, love. For life in perfect whole
And aim consummated, is love in sooth,
As nature's magnet-heat rounds pole with pole.

Ella Wheeler Wilcox
(1850-1919)

I Love You

I love your lips when they're wet with wine
And red with a wild desire;
I love your eyes when the lovelight lies
Lit with a passionate fire.
I love your arms when the warm white flesh
Touches mine in a fond embrace;
I love your hair when the strands enmesh
Your kisses against my face.

Not for me the cold, calm kiss
Of a virgin's bloodless love;
Not for me the saint's white bliss,
Nor the heart of a spotless dove.
But give me the love that so freely gives
And laughs at the whole world's blame,
With your body so young and warm in my arms,
It sets my poor heart aflame.

So kiss me sweet with your warm wet mouth,
Still fragrant with ruby wine,
And say with a fervor born of the South
That your body and soul are mine.
Clasp me close in your warm young arms,
While the pale stars shine above,
And we'll live our whole young lives away
In the joys of a living love.

Ella Wheeler Wilcox
(1850-1919)

How does Love speak?

How does Love speak?
In the faint flush upon the telltale cheek,
And in the pallor that succeeds it; by
The quivering lid of an averted eye—
The smile that proves the parent to a sigh
Thus doth Love speak.

How does Love speak?
By the uneven heart-throbs, and the freak
Of bounding pulses that stand still and ache,
While new emotions, like strange barges, make
Along vein-channels their disturbing course;
Still as the dawn, and with the dawn's swift force—
Thus doth Love speak.

How does Love speak?
In the avoidance of that which we seek—
The sudden silence and reserve when near—
The eye that glistens with an unshed tear—
The joy that seems the counterpart of fear,
As the alarmèd heart leaps in the breast,
And knows and names and greets its godlike
    guest—
Thus doth Love speak.

Ella Wheeler Wilcox
(1850-1919)

[...]

How does Love speak?
In the proud spirit suddenly grown meek—
The haughty heart grown humble; in the tender
And unnamed light that floods the world with
    splendor;
In the resemblance which the fond eyes trace.

In all fair things to one belovèd face;
In the shy touch of hands that thrill and tremble;
In looks and lips that can no more dissemble—
Thus doth Love speak.

How does Love speak?
In the wild words that uttered seem so weak
They shrink ashamed in silence; in the fire
Glance strikes with glance, swift flashing high and
    higher,
Like lightnings that precede the mighty storm;
In the deep, soulful stillness; in the warm,
Impassioned tide that sweeps through throbbing
    veins,
Between the shores of keen delights and pains;
In the embrace where madness melts in bliss,
And in the convulsive rapture of a kiss—
Thus doth Love speak.

Emily Brontë
(1818-1848)

Love and Friendship

Love is like the wild rose-briar,
Friendship like the holly-tree—
The holly is dark when the rose-briar blooms
But which will bloom most constantly?

The wild rose-briar is sweet in spring,
Its summer blossoms scent the air;
Yet wait till winter comes again
And who will call the wild-briar fair?

Then scorn the silly rose-wreath now
And deck thee with the holly's sheen,
That when December blights thy brow
He still may leave thy garland green.

Emily Dickenson
(1830-1886)

That I Did Always Love

That I did always love
I bring thee Proof
That till I loved
I never lived—Enough—
That I shall love always—
I argue thee
That love is life—
And life hath Immortality—

This—dost thou doubt—Sweet—
Then have I
Nothing to show
But Calvary—

Emily Dickinson
(1830-1886)

Life, XXVIII

I bring an unaccustomed wine
To lips long parching
Next to mine,
And summon them to drink;

Crackling with fever, they Essay,
I turn my brimming eyes away,
And come next hour to look.

The hands still hug the tardy glass—
The lips I would have cooled, alas—
Are so superfluous Cold—

I would as soon attempt to warm
The bosoms where the frost has lain
Ages beneath the mould—

Some other thirsty there may be
To whom this would have pointed me
Had it remained to speak—

And so I always bear the cup
If, haply, mine may be the drop
Some pilgrim thirst to slake—

If, haply, any say to me
"Unto the little, unto me,"
When I at last awake.

Emily Dickinson
(1830-1886)

Wild nights!

Wild nights! Wild nights!
Were I with thee,
Wild nights should be
Our luxury!

Futile the winds
To a heart in port,
Done with the compass,
Done with the chart.

Rowing in Eden!
Ah! the sea!
Might I but moor
Tonight in thee!

Emma Lazarus
(1849-1887)

Venus of the Louvre

Down the long hall she glistens like a star,
The foam-born mother of Love, transfixed to stone,
Yet none the less immortal, breathing on.
Time's brutal hand hath maimed but could not mar.
When first the enthralled enchantress from afar
Dazzled mine eyes, I saw not her alone,
Serenely poised on her world-worshipped throne,
As when she guided once her dove-drawn car,—
But at her feet a pale, death-stricken Jew,
Her life adorer, sobbed farewell to love.
Here *Heine* wept! Here still he weeps anew,
Nor ever shall his shadow lift or move,
While mourns one ardent heart, one poet-brain,
For vanished Hellas and Hebraic pain.

Esther Johnson
(1681-1728)

On Jealousy

Oh, shield me from his rage, celestial Powers!
This tyrant that embitters all my hours
Ah! Love, you've poorly played the monarc's part:
You conquered, but you can't defend, my heart.
So blessed was I throughout thy happy reign,
I thought this monster banished from thy train;
But you would raise him to support your throne,
And now he claims your empire as his own:
Or tell me, tyrants, have you both agreed
That where one reigns the other shall succeed?

Lord George Gordon Byron
(1788-1824)

Stanzas for Music

There be none of Beauty's daughters
With a magic like thee;
And like music on the waters
Is thy sweet voice to me:
When, as if its sound were causing
The charmed ocean's pausing,
The waves lie still and gleaming,
And the lulled winds seem dreaming:

And the midnight moon is weaving
Her bright chain o'er the deep;
Whose breast is gently heaving,
As an infant's asleep:
So the spirit bows before thee,
To listen and adore thee;
With a full but soft emotion,
Like the swell of Summer's ocean.

Lord George Gordon Byron
(1788-1824)

She Walks in Beauty

She walks in beauty, like the night
Of cloudless climes and starry skies;
And all that's best of dark and bright
Meet in her aspect and her eyes;
Thus mellowed to that tender light
Which heaven to gaudy day denies.

One shade the more, one ray the less,
Had half impaired the nameless grace
Which waves in every raven tress,
Or softly lightens o'er her face;
Where thoughts serenely sweet express,
How pure, how dear their dwelling-place.

And on that cheek, and o'er that brow,
So soft, so calm, yet eloquent,
The smiles that win, the tints that glow,
But tell of days in goodness spent,
A mind at peace with all below,
A heart whose love is innocent!

Lord George Gordon Byron
(1788-1824)

Love and Death

I watched thee when the foe was at our side,
Ready to strike at him—or thee and me,
Were safety hopeless—rather than divide
Aught with one loved save love and liberty.
I watched thee on the breakers, when the rock,
Received our prow, and all was storm and fear,
And bade thee cling to me through every shock;
This arm would be thy bark, or breast thy bier.

I watched thee when the fever glazed thine eyes,
Yielding my couch and stretched me on the
  ground
When overworn with watching, ne'er to rise
From thence if thou an early grave hadst found.
The earthquake came, and rocked the quivering
  wall,
And men and nature reeled as if with wine.
Whom did I seek around the tottering hall?
For thee. Whose safety first provide for? Thine.
And when convulsive throes denied my breath
The faintest utterance to my fading thought,
To thee—to thee—even in the gasp of death
My spirit turned, oh! oftener than it ought.

Lord George Gordon Byron
(1788-1824)

[...]

Thus much and more; and yet thou lov'st me not,
And never wilt! Love dwells not in our will.
Nor can I blame thee, though it be my lot
To strongly, wrongly, vainly love thee still.

George Eliot

(1819-1880)

Felix Holt, The Radical

Why, there are maidens of heroic touch
And yet they seem like things of gossamer
You'd pinch the life out of, as out of moths.
O, it is not fond tones and mouthingness,
'Tis not the arms akimbo and large strides,
That makes a woman's force. The tiniest birds,
With softest downy breasts, have passion in them,
And are brave with love.

Sir George Etherege
(1635-1692)

Sylvia

The Nymph that undoes me, is fair and unkind;
No less than a wonder by Nature designed.
She's the grief of my heart, the joy of my eye;
And the cause of a flame that never can die!
Her mouth, from whence wit still obligingly flows,
Has the beautiful blush, and the smell, of the rose.
Love and Destiny both attend on her will;
She wounds with a look; with a frown, she can kill!
The desperate Lover can hope no redress;
Where Beauty and Rigour are both in excess!
In Sylvia they meet; so unhappy am I!
Who sees her, must love; and who loves her, must
    die!

George Herbert
(1593-1633)

The Pearl

MATTHEW xiii

I know the ways of learning; both the head
And pipes that feed the press, and make it run;
What reason hath from nature borrowed,
Or of itself, like a good housewife, spun
In laws and policy; what the stars conspire,
What willing nature speaks, what forced by fire;
Both the old discoveries and the new-found seas,
The stock and surplus, cause and history;
All these stand open, or I have the keys:
Yet I love thee.

I know the ways of honour; what maintains
The quick returns of courtesy and wit;
In vies of favours whether party gains
When glory swells the heart and moldeth it
To all expressions both of hand and eye,
Which on the world a true-love-knot may tie,
And bear the bundle wheresoe'er it goes;
How many drams of spirit there must be
To sell my life unto my friends or foes:
Yet I love thee.

I know the ways of pleasure; the sweet strains
The lullings and the relishes of it;
The propositions of hot blood and brains;
What mirth and music mean; what love and wit
Have done these twenty hundred years and more;
I know the projects of unbridled store;

George Herbert
(1593-1633)

[...]

My stuff is flesh, not brass; my senses live,
And grumble oft that they have more in me
Than he that curbs them, being but one to five:
Yet I love thee.
I know all these and have them in my hand;
Therefore not sealed but with open eyes
I fly to thee, and fully understand
Both the main sale and the commodities;
And at what rate and price I have thy love,
With all the circumstances that may move.
Yet through the labyrinths, not my grovelling wit,
But thy silk twist let down from heaven to me
Did both conduct and teach me how by it
To climb to thee.

George Herbert
(1593-1633)

The Agony

Philosophers have measured mountains,
Fathomed the depths of seas, of states, and kings,
Walked with a staff to heaven, and traced
  fountains:
But there are two vast, spacious things,
The which to measure it doth more behove:
Yet few there are that sound them; sin and love.

Who would know sin, let him repair
Unto Mount Olivet; there shall he see
A man so wrung with pains, that all his hair,
His skin, his garments bloody be.
Sin is that press and vice, which forceth pain
To hunt his cruel food through every vein.

Who knows not love, let him assay
And taste that juice, which on the crosse a pike
Did set again abroach; then let him say
If ever he did taste the like.
Love is that liquour sweet and most divine,
Which my God feels as blood; but I, as wine.

George Meredith
(1828-1909)

Modern Love: XXIX

Am I failing? For no longer can I cast
A glory round about this head of gold.
Glory she wears, but springing from the mould;
Not like the consecration of the Past!
Is my soul beggared? Something more than earth
I cry for still: I cannot be at peace
In having Love upon a mortal lease.
I cannot take the woman at her worth!
Where is the ancient wealth wherewith I clothed
Our human nakedness, and could endow
With spiritual splendour a white brow
That else had grinned at me the fact I loathed?
A kiss is but a kiss now! and no wave
Of a great flood that whirls me to the sea.
But, as you will! We'll sit contentedly,
And eat our pot of honey on the grave.

Gustavo Bécquer
(1836-1870)

Rhyme IX

Softly moaning the dawn
kisses the gentle waves as it tousles them playfully;
the sun kisses the clouds in the West
and shades them purple and gold;
the flame slips behind the burning trunk
to kiss another flame;
and even the willow, leaning under its own weight
towards the river, returns its kiss.

Gustavo Bécquer
(1836-1870)

Rhyme XIII

Your eyes are blue and when you laugh
their smooth clarity
reminds me of the morning's tremulous glow
reflected in the sea.

Your eyes are blue and when you cry
their transparent tears
seem like dew drops
resting on a violet.

Your eyes are blue and when from deep down
they radiate an idea like a speck of light
they seem like a lost star
in the evening sky.

Harry Graham
(1874-1936)

Opportunity

When Mrs Gorm (Aunt Eloïse)
was stung to death by savage bees
her husband (Prebendary Gorm)
put on his veil, and took the swarm.
He's publishing a book, next May,
on "How to make bee-keeping pay."

Harry Graham
(1874-1936)

Tragedy

That morning, when my wife eloped
with James, our chauffeur, how I moped!
What tragedies in life there are!
I'm dashed if I can start the car.

Herbert Trench
(1865-1923)

She Comes Not When Noon is
   on the Roses

She comes not when noon is on the roses—
   Too bright is day.
She comes not to the soul till it reposes
   From work and play.

But when night is on the hills, and the great voices
   Roll in from the sea,
By starlight and by candlelight and dreamlight
   She comes to me.

James Thomson
(1834-1882)

Sunday Up the River, Part XVIII

The wine of love is music,
And the feast of love is song:
And when Love sits down to the banquet,
Love sits long:

Sits long and rises drunken,
But not with the feast and the wine;
He reeleth with his own heart,
That great, rich vine.

John Boyle O'Reilly
(1844-1890)

The White Rose

The red rose whispers of passion,
And the white rose breathes of love;
O, the red rose is a falcon,
And the white rose is a dove.

But I send you a cream-white rosebud
With a flush on its petal tips;
For the love that is purest and sweetest
Has a kiss of desire on the lips.

John Clare

(1793-1864)

A Spring Morning

The spring comes in with all her hues and smells,
In freshness breathing over hills and dells;
O'er woods where May her gorgeous drapery flings,
And mead washed fragrant by their laughing
    springs.
Fresh are new opened flowers, untouched and free
From the bold rifling of the amorous bee.
The happy time of singing birds is come,
And love's lone pilgrimage now finds a home;
Amount the mossy oaks now coos the dove,
And the hoarse crow finds softer notes to love.
The foxes play around their dens, and bark
In joy's excess, 'mid woodland shadows dark.
The flowers join lips below; the leaves above;
And every sound that meets the ear is love.

John Clare
(1793-1864)

First Love

I ne'er was struck before that hour
  With love so sudden and so sweet,
Her face it bloomed like a sweet flower
  And stole my heart away complete.
My face turned pale as deadly pale,
  My legs refused to walk away,
And when she looked, what could I ail?
  My life and all seemed turned to clay.

And then my blood rushed to my face
  And took my eyesight quite away,
The trees and bushes round the place
  Seemed midnight at noonday.
I could not see a single thing,
  Words from my eyes did start—
They spoke as chords do from the string,
  And blood burnt round my heart.

Are flowers the winter's choice?
  Is love's bed always snow?
She seemed to hear my silent voice,
  Not love's appeals to know.
I never saw so sweet a face
  As that I stood before.
My heart has left its dwelling-place
  And can return no more.

John Clare
(1793-1864)

I am

I am—yet what I am none cares or knows;
My friends forsake me like a memory lost:
I am the self-consumer of my woes—
They rise and vanish in oblivious host,
Like shadows in love's frenzied stifled throes
And yet I am, and live—like vapours tossed

Into the nothingness of scorn and noise,
Into the living sea of waking dreams,
Where there is neither sense of life or joys,
But the vast shipwreck of my life's esteems;
Even the dearest that I loved the best
Are strange—nay, rather, stranger than the rest.

I long for scenes where man hath never trod
A place where woman never smiled or wept
There to abide with my Creator, God,
And sleep as I in childhood sweetly slept,
Untroubling and untroubled where I lie
The grass below—above the vaulted sky.

John Cornford
(1915-1936)

To Margot Heinemann

Heart of the heartless world,
Dear heart, the thought of you
Is the pain at my side,
The shadow that chills my view.

The wind rises in the evening,
Reminds that autumn is near.
I am afraid to lose you,
I am afraid of my fear.

On the last mile to Huesca,
The last fence for our pride,
Think so kindly, dear, that I
Sense you at my side.

And if bad luck should lay my strength
Into the shallow grave,
Remember all the good you can;
Don't forget my love.

John Donne
(1572-1631)

The Good Morrow

I wonder, by my troth, what thou and I
Did, till we loved? Were we not weaned till then?
But sucked on country pleasures, childishly?
Or snorted we in the Seven Sleepers' den?
'Twas so; but this, all pleasures fancies be.

If ever any beauty I did see,
Which I desired, and got, 'twas but a dream of thee.
And now good-morrow to our waking souls,
Which watch not one another out of fear;
For love, all love of other sights controls,
And makes one little room an everywhere.

Let sea-discoverers to new worlds have gone,
Let maps to other, worlds on worlds have shown,
Let us possess one world, each hath one, and is one.
My face in thine eye, thine in mine appears,
And true plain hearts do in the faces rest;
Where can we find two better hemispheres,
Without sharp north, without declining west?
Whatever dies, was not mixed equally;
If our two loves be one, or, thou and I
Love so alike, that none do slacken, none can die.

John Donne
(1572-1631)

The Sun Rising

Busy old fool, unruly Sun,
Why dost thou thus,
Through windows, and through curtains call on
   us?
Must to thy motions lovers seasons run?
Saucy pedantic wretch, go chide
Late school boys, and sour prentices,
Go tell court-huntsmen, that the King will ride,
Call country ants to harvest offices;
Love, all alike, no season knows, nor clime,
Nor hours, days, months, which are the rags of
   time.

Thy beams, so reverend, and strong
Why shouldst thou think?
I could eclipse and cloud them with a wink,
But that I would not lose her sight so long:
If her eyes have not blinded thine,
Look, and tomorrow late, tell me,
Whether both the Indias of spice and mine
Be where thou leftst them, or lie here with me.
Ask for those kings whom thou saw'st yesterday,
And thou shalt hear, all here in one bed lay.

John Donne
(1572-1631)

[...]

She's all states, and all princes, I,
Nothing else is.
Princes do but play us; compared to this,
All honor's mimic; all wealth alchemy.
Thou sun art half as happy as we,
In that the world's contracted thus;
Thine age asks ease, and since thy duties be
To warm the world, that's done in warming us.
Shine here to us, and thou art everywhere;
This bed thy center is, these walls, thy sphere.

John Donne

(1572-1631)

The Flea

Mark but this flea, and mark in this,
How little that which thou deniest me is;
It sucked me first, and now sucks thee,
And in this flea our two bloods mingled be.
Thou knowest that this cannot be said
A sin, nor shame, nor loss of maidenhead;
Yet this enjoys before it woo,
And pampered swells with one blood made of two;
And this, alas, is more than we would do.

O stay, three lives in one flea spare,
Where we almost, yea, more than married are.
This flea is you and I, and this
Our marriage bed, and marriage temple is.
Though parents grudge, and you, we're met,
And cloistered in these living walls of jet.
Though use make you apt to kill me,
Let not to that self-murder added be,
And sacrilege, three sins in killing three.

Cruel and sudden, hast thou since
Purpled thy nail in blood of innocence?
Wherein could this flea guilty be,
Except in that drop which it sucked from thee?
Yet thou triumphest, and sayest that thou
Find'st not thyself nor me the weaker now.
'Tis true; then learn how false fears be;
Just so much honour, when thou yield'st to me
Will waste, as this flea's death took life from thee.

John Dryden
(1631-1700)

Ah, How Sweet It Is To Love!

Ah, how sweet it is to love!
Ah, how gay is young desire!
And what pleasing pains we prove
When we first approach Love's fire!
Pains of love be sweeter far
Than all other pleasures are.

Sighs which are from lovers blown
Do but gently heave the heart:
Even the tears they shed alone
Cure, like trickling balm, their smart:
Lovers, when they lose their breath,
Bleed away in easy death.

Love and time with reverence use,
Treat them like a parting friend;
Nor the golden gifts refuse
Which in youth sincere they send:
For each year their price is more,
And they less simple than before.

Love, like spring-tides full and high,
Swells in every youthful vein;
But each tide does less supply,
Till they quite shrink in again:
If a flow in age appear,
'Tis but rain, and runs not clear.

John Dryden
(1631-1700)

Song

Sylvia the fair, in the bloom of fifteen,
Felt an innocent warmth as she lay on the green:
She had heard of a pleasure, and something she
   guessed
By the towsing and tumbling and touching her
   breast:
She saw the men eager, but was at a loss
What they meant by their sighing and kissing so
   close;
By their praying and whining,
And clasping and twining,
And panting and wishing,
And sighing and kissing,
And sighing and kissing so close.

"Ah!" she cried, "ah, for a languishing maid
In a country of Christians to die without aid!
Not a Whig, or a Tory, or Trimmer at least,
Or a Protestant parson, or Catholic priest,
To instruct a young virgin that is at a loss
What they meant by their sighing and kissing so
   close;
By their praying and whining,
And clasping and twining,
And panting and wishing,
And sighing and kissing,
And sighing and kissing so close."

John Dryden
(1631-1700)

[...]

Cupid in shape of a swain did appear;
He saw the sad wound, and in pity drew near;
Then showed her his arrow, and bid her not fear,
For the pain was no more than a maiden may bear;
When the balm was infused, she was not at a loss
What they meant by their sighing and kissing so
  close;
By their praying and whining,
And clasping and twining,
And panting and wishing,
And sighing and kissing,
And sighing and kissing so close.

John Fletcher

(1579-1625)

Love's Emblems

Now the lusty spring is seen;
  Golden yellow, gaudy blue,
  Daintily invite the view:
Everywhere on every green
Roses blushing as they blow
  And enticing men to pull,
Lilies whiter than the snow,
  Woodbines of sweet honey full:
    All love's emblems, and all cry,
    "Ladies, if not plucked, we die."

Yet the lusty spring hath stayed;
  Blushing red and purest white
  Daintily to love invite
Every woman, every maid:
Cherries kissing as they grow,
  And inviting men to taste,
Apples even ripe below,
  Winding gently to the waist:
    All love's emblems, and all cry,
    "Ladies, if not plucked, we die."

John Fletcher
(1579-1625)

Beauty Clear and Fair

Beauty clear and fair,
  Where the air
Rather like a perfume dwells;
  Where the violet and the rose
  Their blue veins and blush disclose,
And come to honour nothing else:

  Where to live near
  And planted there
Is to live, and still live new;
  Where to gain a favour is
  More than light, perpetual bliss--
Make me live by serving you!

Dear, again back recall
  To this light,
A stranger to himself and all!
  Both the wonder and the story
  Shall be yours, and eke the glory;
I am your servant, and your thrall.

John Fletcher
(1579-1625)

Take, oh, take those lips away

Take, oh, take those lips away
That so sweetly were forsworn
And those eyes, like break of day,
Lights that do mislead the morn;
But my kisses bring again,
Seals of love, though sealed in vain.

Hide, oh, hide those hills of snow,
Which thy frozen bosom bears,
On whose tops the pinks that grow
Are of those that April wears;
But first set my poor heart free,
Bound in those icy chains by thee.

John Keats
(1792-1821)

Bright Star

Bright star, would I were stedfast as thou art—
    Not in lone splendour hung aloft the night
And watching, with eternal lids apart,
    Like nature's patient, sleepless Eremite,
The moving waters at their priestlike task
    Of pure ablution round earth's human shores,
Or gazing on the new soft-fallen mask
    Of snow upon the mountains and the moors—
No—yet still stedfast, still unchangeable,
    Pillowed upon my fair love's ripening breast,
To feel for ever its soft fall and swell,
    Awake for ever in a sweet unrest,
Still, still to hear her tender-taken breath,
And so live ever—or else swoon to death.

John Keats
(1792-1821)

Give Me Women, Wine and Snuff

Give me women, wine, and snuff
Untill I cry out "hold, enough!"
You may do so sans objection
Till the day of resurrection:
For, bless my beard, they aye shall be
My beloved Trinity.

John Keats
(1792-1821)

The Day is Gone

The day is gone, and all its sweets are gone!
Sweet voice, sweet lips, soft hand, and softer
    breast,
Warm breath, light whisper, tender semi-tone,
Bright eyes, accomplished shape, and langourous
    waist!
Faded the flower and all its budded charms,
Faded the sight of beauty from my eyes,
Faded the shape of beauty from my arms,
Faded the voice, warmth, whiteness, paradise–
Vanished unseasonably at shut of eve,
When the dusk holiday–or holinight
Of fragrant-curtained love begins to weave
The woof of darkness thick, for hid delight,
But, as I've read love's missal through to-day,
He'll let me sleep, seeing I fast and pray.

John Millington Synge
(1871-1909)

In May

In a nook
that opened south,
You and I
Lay mouth to mouth.

A snowy gull
And sooty daw
Came and looked
With many a caw

"Such," I said,
"Are I and You,
When you've kissed me
Black and blue!"

John Millington Synge
(1871-1909)

Is It A Month?

Is it a month since I and you
In the starlight of Glen Dubh
Stretched beneath a hazel bough
Kissed from ear to throat to brow,
Since your fingers, neck and chin
Made the bars that fenced me in,
Till Paradise seemed but a wreck?
Near your bosom, brow and neck
And stars grew wilder, growing wise
In the splendour of your eyes!

Since the weasel wandered near
Whilst we kissed from ear to ear
And the wet and withered leaves
Blew about your cap and sleeves,
Till the moon sank tired through the edge
Of the wet and windy hedge?
And we took the starry lane
Back to Dublin town again.

John Wilbye
(1574-1638)

Love Not Me For Comely Grace

Love not me for comely grace,
For me pleasing eye or face,
Nor for any outward part,
No, nor for a constant heart:
For these may fail or turn to ill,
So thou and I shall sever:
Keep, therefore, a true woman's eye,
And love me still but not know why–
So hast thou the same reason still
To dote upon me ever!

John Wilmot, Earl of Rochester
(1647-1680)

The Imperfect Enjoyment

Naked she lay, clasped in my longing arms,
I filled with love, and she all over charms;
Both equally inspired with eager fire,
Melting through kindness, flaming in desire;
With arms, legs, lips close clinging to embrace,
She clips me to her breast and sucks me to her face.
Her nimble tongue, (love's lesser lightning), played
Within my mouth and to my thoughts conveyed
Swift orders that I should prepare to throw
The all-dissolving thunderbolt below.
My fluttering soul, sprung with the painted kiss,
Hangs hovering o'er her balmy brinks of bliss.
But whilst her busy hand would guide that part
Which should convey my soul up to her heart,
In liquid raptures I dissolve all o'er,
Melt into sperm, and spend at every pore.
A touch from any part of her had done't,
Her hand, her foot, her very look's a cunt.
Smiling, she chides in a kind murmuring noise,
And from her body wipes the clammy joys,
When, with a thousand kisses wandering o'er
My panting bosom, "Is there then no more?"
She cries, "All this to love and rapture's due;
Must we not pay a debt to pleasure too?"
But I, the most forlorn, lost man alive,
To show my wished obedience vainly strive,
I sigh, alas, and kiss, but cannot swive.
Eager desires confound my first intent,
Succeeding shame does more success prevent,
And rage at last confirms me impotent.

John Wilmot, Earl of Rochester
(1647-1680)

[...]

Even her fair hand, which might bid heat return
To frozen age, and make cold hermits burn,
Applied to my dead cinder, warms no more
Than fire to ashes could past flames restore.
Trembling, confused, despairing, limber, dry,
A wishing, weak, unmoving lump I lie.
This dart of Love, whose piercing point, oft tried,
With virgin blood ten thousand maids have dyed;
Which nature still directed with such art
That it through every cunt reached every heart —
Stiffly resolved, 'twould carelessly invade
Woman or boy, nor ought its fury stayed:
Where'er it pierced, a cunt it found or made —
Now languid lies in this unhappy hour,
Shrunk up and sapless like a withered flower.
Thou treacherous, base deserter of my flame,
False to my passion, fatal to my fame,
By what mistaken magic dost thou prove
So true to lewdness, so untrue to love?
What oyster, cinder, beggar, common whore
Didst thou ever fail in all thy life before?
When vice, disease, and scandal lead the way,
With what officious haste dost thou obey!
Like a rude, roaring hector in the streets
Who scuffles, cuffs, and justles all he meets,
But if his king or country claim his aid,
The rakehell villain shrinks and hides his head;
Even so thy brutal valour is displayed,
Breaks every stew, does each small whore invade,

John Wilmot, Earl of Rochester
(1647-1680)

[...]

But when great Love the onset does command,
Base recreant to thy prince, thou dar'st not stand.
Worst part of me, and henceforth hated most,
Through all the town a common fucking post,
On whom each whore relieves her tingling cunt
As hogs do rub themselves on gates and grunt,
May'st thou to ravenous chancres be a prey,
Or in consuming weepings waste away.
May strangury and stone thy days attend;
May'st thou ne'er piss, who did refuse to spend
When all my joys did on false thee depend.
And may ten thousand abler pricks agree
To do the wronged Corinna right for thee.

John Wilmot, Earl of Rochester
(1647-1680)

To His Mistress

Why dost thou shade thy lovely face? O why
Does that eclipsing hand of thine deny
The sunshine of the sun's enlivening eye?

Without thy light what light remains in me?
Thou art my life; my way, my light's in thee;
I live, I move, and by thy beams I see.

Thou art my life-if thou but turn away
My life's a thousand deaths. Thou art my way-
Without thee, love, I travel not but stray.

My light thou art-without thy glorious sight
My eyes are darkened with eternal night.
My love, thou art my way, my life, my light.

Thou art my way; I wander if thou fly.
Thou art my light; if hid, how blind am I!
Thou art my life; if thou withdraw'st, I die.

My eyes are dark and blind, I cannot see:
To whom or whither should my darkness flee,
But to that light?- and who's that light but thee?

If I have lost my path, dear lover, say,
Shall I still wander in a doubtful way?
Love, shall a lamb of Israel's sheepfold stray?

John Wilmot, Earl of Rochester
(1647-1680)

[...]

My path is lost, my wandering steps do stray;
I cannot go, nor can I safely stay;
Whom should I seek but thee, my path, my way?

And yet thou turn'st thy face away and fly'st me!
And yet I sue for grace and thou deny'st me!
Speak, art thou angry, Love, or only try'st me?

Thou art the pilgrim's path, the blind man's eye,
The dead man's life. On thee my hopes rely:
If I but them remove, I surely die.

Dissolve thy sunbeams, close thy wings and stay!
See, see how I am blind, and dead, and stray!
—O thou art my life, my light, my way!

Then work thy will! If passion bid me flee,
My reason shall obey, my wings shall be
Stretched out no farther than from me to thee!

John Wilmot, Earl of Rochester
(1647-1680)

A Song of a Young Lady to Her
Ancient Lover

Ancient person, for whom I
All the flattering youth defy,
Long be it ere thou grow old,
Aching, shaking, crazy, cold;
But still continue as thou art,
Ancient person of my heart.

On thy withered lips and dry,
Which like barren furrows lie,
Brooding kisses I will pour
Shall thy youthful heat restore
(Such kind showers in autumn fall,
And a second spring recall);
Nor from thee will ever part,
Ancient person of my heart.

Thy nobler part, which but to name
In our sex would be counted shame,
By age's frozen grasp possess,
From his ice shall be released,
And soothed by my reviving hand,
In former warmth and vigor stand.
All a lover's wish can reach
For thy joy my love shall teach,
And for they pleasure shall improve
All that art can add to love.
Yet still I love thee without art,
Ancient person of my heart.

Jonathan Swift
(1667-1745)

Stella's Birthday March 13, 1719

Stella this day is thirty-four,
(We shan't dispute a year or more:)
However, Stella, be not troubled,
Although thy size and years are doubled,
Since first I saw thee at sixteen,
The brightest virgin on the green;
So little is thy form declined;
Made up so largely in thy mind.

Oh, would it please the gods to split
Thy beauty, size, and years, and wit;
No age could furnish out a pair
Of nymphs so graceful, wise, and fair;
With half the lustre of your eyes,
With half your wit, your years, and size.
And then, before it grew too late,
How should I beg of gentle Fate,
(That either nymph might have her swain,)
To split my worship too in twain.

Jonathan Swift
(1667-1745)

To Stella on Her Birthday, 1722

While, Stella, to your lasting praise
The Muse her annual tribute pays,
While I assign myself a task
Which you expect, but scorn to ask;
If I perform this task with pain,
Let me of partial fate complain;
You every year the debt enlarge,
I grow less equal to the charge:
In you each virtue brighter shines,
But my poetic vein declines;
My harp will soon in vain be strung,
And all your virtues left unsung.
For none among the upstart race
Of poets dare assume my place;
Your worth will be to them unknown,
They must have Stellas of their own;
And thus, my stock of wit decayed,
I dying leave the debt unpaid,
Unless Delany, as my heir,
Will answer for the whole arrear.

Jonathan Swift
(1667-1745)

Stella's Birthday March 13, 1727

This day, whate'er the Fates decree,
Shall still be kept with joy by me:
This day then let us not be told,
That you are sick, and I grown old;
Nor think on our approaching ills,
And talk of spectacles and pills.
To-morrow will be time enough
To hear such mortifying stuff.
Yet, since from reason may be brought
A better and more pleasing thought,
Which can, in spite of all decays,
Support a few remaining days:
From not the gravest of divines
Accept for once some serious lines.

Athough we now can form no more
Long schemes of life, as heretofore;
Yet you, while time is running fast,
Can look with joy on what is past.

Were future happiness and pain
A mere contrivance of the brain,
As atheists argue, to entice
And fit their proselytes for vice;
(The only comfort they propose,
To have companions in their woes;)
Grant this the case; yet sure 'tis hard
That virtue, styled its own reward,
And by all sages understood
To be the chief of human good,
Should, acting, die, nor leave behind

Jonathan Swift
(1667-1745)

[...]

Some lasting pleasure in the mind;
Which by remembrance will assuage
Grief, sickness, poverty, and age;
And strongly shoot a radiant dart
To shine through life's declining part.

Say, Stella, feel you no content,
Reflecting on a life well spent?
Your skilful hand employed to save
Despairing wretches from the grave;
And then supporting with your store
Those whom you dragged from death before?
So Providence on mortals waits,
Preserving what it first creates.
Your generous boldness to defend
An innocent and absent friend;
That courage which can make you just
To merit humbled in the dust;
The detestation you express
For vice in all its glittering dress;
That patience under torturing pain,
Where stubborn stoics would complain:
Must these like empty shadows pass,
Or forms reflected from a glass?
Or mere chimæras in the mind,
That fly, and leave no marks behind?
Does not the body thrive and grow
By food of twenty years ago?
And, had it not been still supplied,
It must a thousand times have died.
Then who with reason can maintain

Jonathan Swift
(1667-1745)

[...]

That no effects of food remain?
And is not virtue in mankind
The nutriment that feeds the mind;
Upheld by each good action past,
And still continued by the last?
Then, who with reason can pretend
That all effects of virtue end?

Believe me, Stella, when you show
That true contempt for things below,
Nor prize your life for other ends,
Than merely to oblige your friends;
Your former actions claim their part,
And join to fortify your heart.
For Virtue, in her daily race,
Like Janus, bears a double face;
Looks back with joy where she has gone
And therefore goes with courage on:
She at your sickly couch will wait,
And guide you to a better state.

O then, whatever Heaven intends,
Take pity on your pitying friends!
Nor let your ills affect your mind,
To fancy they can be unkind.
Me, surely me, you ought to spare,
Who gladly would your sufferings share;
Or give my scrap of life to you,
And think it far beneath your due;
You, to whose care so oft I owe
That I'm alive to tell you so.

Joseph Mary Plunkett
(1887-1916)

New Love

The day I knew you loved me we had lain
Deep in Coill Doraca down by Gleann na Scath
Unknown to each till suddenly I saw
You in the shadow, knew oppressive pain
Stopping my heart, and there you did remain
In dreadful beauty fair without a flaw,
Blinding the eyes that yet could not withdraw
Till wild between us drove the wind and rain.

Breathless we reached the brugh before the west
Burst in full fury—then with lightning stroke
The tempest in my heart roared up and broke
Its barriers, and I swore I would not rest
Till that mad heart was worthy of your breast
Or dead for you—and then this love awoke.

Joseph Mary Plunkett
(1887-1916)

The Little Black Rose
Shall Be Red At Last

Because we share our sorrows and our joys
And all your dear and intimate thoughts are mine
We shall not fear the trumpets and the noise
Of battle, for we know our dreams divine,
And when my heart is pillowed on your heart
And ebb and flowing of their passionate flood
Shall beat in concord love through every part
Of brain and body—when at last the blood
O'erleaps the final barrier to find
Only one source wherein to spend its strength
And we two lovers, long but one in mind
And soul, are made one only flesh at length;
Praise God if this my blood fulfils the doom
When you, dark rose, shall redden into bloom.

Lady Katherine Dyer
(16??-1674)

Epitaph to her husband
in the church of St Denis
(left-hand side of diptych)

If a large heart, joined with a noble mind
Showing true worth, unto all good inclined
If faith in friendship, justice unto all,
Leave such a memory as we may call
Happy, thine is; then pious marble keep
His just fame waking, though his loved dust sleep.
And though death can devour all it hath breath,
And monuments themselves have had a death,
Nature shan't suffer this, to ruinate,
Nor time demolish it, nor an envious fate,
Raised by a just hand, not vainglorious pride,
Who'd be concealed, were it modesty to hide,
Such an affection did so long survive
The object of it, yet loved it as alive.
And this great blessing to his name doth give
To make it by his tomb, and issue live.

Lady Katherine Dyer
(16??-1674)

Epitaph to her husband
in the church of St Denis
(right-hand side of diptych)

My dearest dust, could not thy hasty day
Afford thy drowsy patience leave to stay
One hour longer: so that we might either
Sat up, or gone to bed together?
But since thy finished labour hath possessed
Thy weary limbs with early rest,
Enjoy it sweetly: and thy widow bride
Shall soon repose her by thy slumbering side.
Whose business, now, is only to prepare
My nightly dress, and call to prayer:
Mine eyes wax heavy and the day grows old.
The dew falls thick, my blood grows cold.
Draw, draw the closed curtains & make room:
My dear, my dearest dust; I come, I come.

Katherine Mansfield
(1888-1923)

Camomile Tea

Outside the sky is light with stars;
There's a hollow roaring from the sea.
And, alas! for the little almond flowers,
The wind is shaking the almond tree.

How little I thought, a year ago,
In the horrible cottage upon the Lee
That he and I should be sitting so
And sipping a cup of camomile tea.

Light as feathers the witches fly,
The horn of the moon is plain to see;
By a firefly under a jonquil flower
A goblin toasts a bumble-bee.

We might be fifty, we might be five,
So snug, so compact, so wise are we!
Under the kitchen-table leg
My knee is pressing against his knee.

Our shutters are shut, the fire is low,
The tap is dripping peacefully;
The saucepan shadows on the wall
Are black and round and plain to see.

Katherine Mansfield
(1888-1923)

Sorrowing Love

And again the flowers are come,
And the light shakes,
And no tiny voice is dumb,
And a bud breaks
On the humble bush and the proud restless tree.
Come with me!

Look, this little flower is pink,
And this one white.
Here's a pearl cup for your drink,
Here's for your delight
A yellow one, sweet with honey.
Here's fairy money
Silver bright
Scattered over the grass
As we pass.

Here's moss. How the smell of it lingers
On my cold fingers!
You shall have no moss. Here's a frail
Hyacinth, deathly pale.
Not for you, not for you!
And the place where they grew
You must promise me not to discover,
My sorrowful lover!
Shall we never be happy again?
Never again play?
In vain--in vain!
Come away!

Katherine Mansfield
(1888-1923)

Covering Wings

Love! Love! Your tenderness,
Your beautiful, watchful ways
Grasp me, fold me, cover me;
I lie in a kind of daze,
Neither asleep nor yet awake,
Neither a bud nor flower.
Brings to-morrow
Joy or sorrow,
The black or the golden hour?

Love! Love! You pity me so!
Chide me, scold me--cry,
"Submit--submit! You must not fight!"
What may I do, then? Die?
But, oh my horror of quiet beds!
How can I longer stay!
"One to be ready,
Two to be steady,
Three to be off and away!"

Darling heart--your gravity!
Your sorrowful, mournful gaze--
"Two bleached roads lie under the moon,
At the parting of the ways."
But the tiny, tree-thatched, narrow lane,
Isn't it yours and mine?
The blue-bells ring
Hey, ding-a-ding, ding!
And buds are thick on the vine.
Love! Love! Grief of my heart!

Katherine Mansfield
(1888-1923)

[...]

As a tree droops over a stream
You hush me, lull me, dark me,
The shadow hiding the gleam.
Your drooping and tragical boughs of grace
Are heavy as though with rain.
Run! Run!
Into the sun!
Let us be children again.

Katherine Philips
(1631-1664)

To One Persuading a Lady to Marriage

Forbear, bold youth, all's Heaven here,
And what you do aver,
To others, courtship may appear,
'Tis sacriledge to her.
She is a publick deity,
And were't not very odd
She should depose herself to be
A petty household god?

First make the sun in private shine,
And bid the world adieu,
That so he may his beams confine
In complement to you.
But if of that you do despair,
Think how you did amiss,
To strive to fix her beams which are
More bright and large than this.

Katherine Philips
(1631-1664)

A Married State

A married state affords but little ease
The best of husbands are so hard to please.
This in wives' careful faces you may spell
Though they dissemble their misfortunes well.
A virgin state is crowned with much content;
It's always happy as it's innocent.
No blustering husbands to create your fears;
No pangs of childbirth to extort your tears;
No children's cries for to offend your ears;
Few worldly crosses to distract your prayers:
Thus are you freed from all the cares that do
Attend on matrimony and a husband too.
Therefore Madam, be advised by me
Turn, turn apostate to love's levity,
Suppress wild nature if she dare rebel.
There's no such thing as leading apes in hell.

Katherine Philips

(1631-1664)

Against Love

Hence Cupid! with your cheating toys
Your real griefs, and painted Joys,
Your pleasure which itself destroys.
Lovers like men in fevers burn and rave,
And only what will injure them do crave.
Men's weakness makes Love so severe,
They give him power by their fear,
And make the shackles which they wear.
Who to another does his heart submit,
Makes his own idol, and then worships it.
Him whose heart is all his own,
Peace and liberty does crown,
He apprehends no killing frown.
He feels no raptures which are joys diseased,
And is not much transported, but still pleased.

Mary Elizabeth Coleridge
(1861-1907)

A Moment

The clouds had made a crimson crown
Above the mountains high.
The stormy sun was going down
In a stormy sky.

Why did you let your eyes so rest on me,
And hold your breath between?
In all the ages this can never be
As if it had not been.

Mary Elizabeth Coleridge
(1861-1907)

Marriage

No more alone sleeping, no more alone waking,
Thy dreams divided, thy prayers in twain;
Thy merry sisters tonight forsaking,
Never shall we see, maiden, again.

Never shall we see thee, thine eyes glancing.
Flashing with laughter and wild in glee,
Under the mistletoe kissing and dancing,
Wantonly free.

There shall come a matron walking sedately,
Low-voiced, gentle, wise in reply.
Tell me, O tell me, can I love her greatly?
All for her sake must the maiden die!

Matthew Arnold
(1822-1888)

Longing

Come to me in my dreams, and then
By day I shall be well again.
For then the night will more than pay
The hopeless longing of the day.

Come, as thou cam'st a thousand times,
A messenger from radiant climes,
And smile on thy new world, and be
As kind to others as to me.

Or, as thou never cam'st in sooth,
Come now, and let me dream it truth.
And part my hair, and kiss my brow,
And say My love! why sufferest thou?

Come to me in my dreams, and then
By day I shall be well again.
For then the night will more than pay
The hopeless longing of the day.

Matthew Arnold
(1822-1888)

Dover Beach

The sea is calm to-night.
The tide is full, the moon lies fair
Upon the straits;—on the French coast the light
Gleams and is gone; the cliffs of England stand,
Glimmering and vast, out in the tranquil bay.
Come to the window, sweet is the night-air!
Only, from the long line of spray
Where the sea meets the moon-blanched land,
Listen! you hear the grating roar
Of pebbles which the waves draw back, and fling,
At their return, up the high strand,
Begin, and cease, and then again begin,
With tremulous cadence slow, and bring
The eternal note of sadness in.

Sophocles long ago
Heard it on the Aegean, and it brought
Into his mind the turbid ebb and flow
Of human misery; we
Find also in the sound a thought,
Hearing it by this distant northern sea.

The Sea of Faith
Was once, too, at the full, and round earth's shore
Lay like the folds of a bright girdle furled.
But now I only hear

Matthew Arnold
(1822-1888)

[...]

Its melancholy, long, withdrawing roar,
Retreating, to the breath
Of the night-wind, down the vast edges drear
And naked shingles of the world.

Ah, love, let us be true
To one another! for the world, which seems
To lie before us like a land of dreams,
So various, so beautiful, so new,
Hath really neither joy, nor love, nor light,
Nor certitude, nor peace, nor help for pain;
And we are here as on a darkling plain
Swept with confused alarms of struggle and
  flight,
Where ignorant armies clash by night.

Michael Drayton

(1563-1631)

Dear, Why Should You Command Me to My Rest?

Dear, why should you command me to my rest
When now the night doth summon all to sleep?
Methinks this time becometh lovers best;
Night was ordained together friends to keep.
How happy are all other living things
Which, though the day disjoin by several flight,
The quiet evening yet together brings,
And each returns unto his love at night!
O thou that art so courteous else to all,
Why should'st thou, Night, abuse me only thus,
That every creature to his kind dost call,
And yet 'tis thou dost only sever us?
Well could I wish it would be ever day,
If when night comes you bid me go away.

Michael Drayton
(1563-1631)

Farewell to Love

Since there's no help, come let us kiss and part;
Nay, I have done, you get no more of me,
And I am glad, yea glad with all my heart
That thus so cleanly I myself can free;
Shake hands forever, cancel all our vows,
And when we meet at any time again,
Be it not seen in either of our brows
That we one jot of former love retain.
Now at the last gasp of Love's latest breath,
When, his pulse failing, Passion speechless lies,
When Faith is kneeling by his bed of death,
And Innocence is closing up his eyes,
Now if thou wouldst, when all have given him
   over,
From death to life thou mightst him yet recover.

Oscar Wilde
(1854-1900)

We are made one with what
we touch and see

We are resolved into the supreme air,
We are made one with what we touch and see,
With our heart's blood each crimson sun is fair,
With our young lives each spring-impassioned tree
Flames into green, the wildest beasts that range
The moor our kinsmen are, all life is one,
   and all is change.

With beat of systole and of diastole
One grand great life throbs through earth's giant
   heart,
And mighty waves of single being roll
From nerve-less germ to man, for we are part
Of every rock and bird and beast and hill,
One with the things that prey on us,
   and one with what we kill . . .

Not we alone hath passions hymeneal,
The yellow buttercups that shake for mirth
At daybreak know a pleasure not less real
Than we do, when in some fresh-blossoming wood
We draw the spring into our hearts,
   and feel that life is good . . .

Is the light vanished from our golden sun,
Or is this daedal-fashioned earth less fair,
That we are nature's heritors, and one

Oscar Wilde
(1854-1900)

[...]

With every pulse of life that beats the air?
Rather new suns across the sky shall pass,
New splendour come unto the flower,
new glory to the grass.

And we two lovers shall not sit afar,
Critics of nature, but the joyous sea
Shall be our raiment, and the bearded star
Shoot arrows at our pleasure! We shall be
Part of the mighty universal whole,
And through all aeons mix
and mingle with the cosmic soul!

We shall be notes in that great symphony
Whose cadence circles through the rhythmic
   spheres,
And all the live world's throbbing heart shall be
One with our heart, the stealthy creeping years
Have lost their terrors now, we shall not die,
The universe itself shall be our immortality!

Percy Bysshe Shelley
(1792-1822)

Love's Philosophy

The fountains mingle with the river
  And the rivers with the ocean,
The winds of heaven mix for ever
  With a sweet emotion;
Nothing in the world is single;
  All things by a law divine
In one spirit meet and mingle.
  Why not I with thine?—

See the mountains kiss high heaven
  And the waves clasp one another;
No sister-flower would be forgiven
  If it disdained its brother;
And the sunlight clasps the earth
  And the moonbeams kiss the sea:
What is all this sweet work worth
  If thou kiss not me?

Percy Bysshe Shelley
(1792-1822)

Music

Music, when soft voices die,
Vibrates in the memory —
Odours, when sweet violets sicken,
Live within the sense they quicken.

Rose leaves, when the rose is dead,
Are heaped for the beloved's bed;
And so thy thoughts when thou are gone,
Love itself shall slumber on.

Sir Philip Sidney
(1554-1586)

My True Love Hath My Heart

My true love hath my heart and I have his,
By just exchange, one for the other given.
I hold his dear, and mine he cannot miss;
There never was a bargain better driven.
His heart in me keeps me and him in one,
My heart in him his thoughts and senses guides;
He loves my heart, for once it was his own,
I cherish his because in me it bides.
His heart his wound received from my sight;,
My heart was wounded with his wounded heart;
For as from me on him his hurt did light,
So still, methought, in me his hurt did smart;
Both equal hurt, in this change sought our bliss:
My true love hath my heart and I have his.

Richard Lovelace
(1617-1657)

Tell Me Not, Sweet

Tell me not, Sweet, I am unkind
For, from the nunnery
Of thy chaste breast, and quiet mind,
To war and arms I fly.

True, a new mistress now I chase,
The first foe in the field;
And with a stronger faith–embrace
A sword, a horse, a shield.

Yet this inconstancy is such
As you too shall adore;
For, I could not love thee, Dear, so much,
Loved I not honour more.

Robert Browning
(1812-1899)

Meeting at Night

The grey sea and the long black land;
And the yellow half-moon large and low
And the startled little waves that leap
In fiery ringlets from their sleep,
As I gain the cove with pushing prow,
And quench its speed in the slushy sand.

Then a mile of warm sea-scented beach;
Three fields to cross till a farm appears;
A tap at the pane, the quick sharp scratch
And blue spurt of a lighted match,
And a voice less loud, through its joys and fears,
Than the two hearts beating each to each!

Robert Browning
(1812-1899)

Life in a Love

Escape me?
Never—
Beloved!
While I am I, and you are you,
So long as the world contains us both,
Me the loving and you the loth,
While the one eludes, must the other pursue.
My life is a fault at last, I fear—
It seems too much like a fate, indeed!
Though I do my best I shall scarce succeed—
But what if I fail of my purpose here?

It is but to keep the nerves at strain,
To dry one's eyes and laugh at a fall,
And baffled, get up to begin again,—
So the chase takes up one's life, that's all.
While, look but once from your farthest bound,
At me so deep in the dust and dark,
No sooner the old hope drops to ground
Than a new one, straight to the selfsame mark,
I shape me—
Ever
Removed!

Robert Browning
(1812-1899)

A Face

If one could have that little head of hers
Painted upon a background of pale gold,
Such as the Tuscan's early art prefers!
No shade encroaching on the matchless mould
Of those two lips, which should be opening soft
In the pure profile; not as when she laughs,
For that spoils all: but rather as if aloft
Yon hyacinth, she loves so, leaned its staff's
Burthen of honey-coloured buds to kiss
And capture 'twixt the lips apart for this.
Then her lithe neck, three fingers might surround,
How it should waver on the pale gold ground,
Up to the fruit-shaped, perfect chin it lifts!
I know, Correggio loves to mass, in rifts
Of heaven, his angel faces, orb on orb
Breaking its outline, burning shades absorb:
But these are only massed there, I should think,
Waiting to see some wonder momently
Grow out, stand full, fade slow against the sky
(That's the pale ground you'd see this sweet face by),
All heaven, meanwhile, condensed into one eye
Which fears to lose the wonder, should it wink.

Robert Burns
(1759-1796)

A Red, Red Rose

O my Luve is like a red, red rose
  That's newly sprung in June:
O my Luve is like the melodie
  That's sweetly played in tune!

So fair art thou, my bonnie lass,
  So deep in luve am I:
And I will luve thee still, my dear,
  Till all the seas gang dry.

Till all the seas gang dry, my dear,
  And the rocks melt with the sun;
I will luve thee still, my dear,
  While the sands o' life shall run.

And fare thee weel, my only Luve,
  And fare thee weel awhile!
And I will come again, my Luve,
  Though it were ten thousand mile.

Robert Herrick
(1591-1674)

To the Virgins, to Make Much of Time

Gather ye rose-buds while ye may,
Old Time is still a-flying;
And this same flower that smiles today
Tomorrow will be dying.

The glorious lamp of heaven, the sun,
The higher he's a-getting,
The sooner will his race be run,
And nearer he's to setting.

That age is best which is the first,
When youth and blood are warmer;
But being spent, the worse, and worst
Times still succeed the former.

Then be not coy, but use your time,
And while ye may, go marry;
For having lost but once your prime,
You may forever tarry.

Robert Herrick
(1591-1674)

Upon Julia's Clothes

Whenas in silks my Julia goes,
Then, then (methinks) how sweetly flows
That liquefaction of her clothes.

Next, when I cast mine eyes, and see
That brave vibration each way free,
O how that glittering taketh me!

Robert Herrick

(1591-1674)

Upon Julia's Breasts

Display thy breasts, my Julia, there let me
Behold that circummortal purity;
Between whose glories, there my lips I'll lay,
Ravished in that fair *Via Lactea*.

Samuel Butler

(1613-1680)

Genuine Remains

All love at first, like generous wine,
Ferments and frets, until 'tis fine;
But when 'tis settled on the lee,
And from the impurer matter free,
Becomes the richer still, the older,
And process the pleasanter, the colder.

Samuel Taylor Coleridge
(1772-1834)

Love

And in life's noisiest hour,
There whispers still the ceaseless love of thee,
The heart's self-solace and soliloquy.
You mould my hopes, you fashion me within ;
And to the leading love-throb in the heart
Through all my being, through my pulse's beat ;
You lie in all my many thoughts, like light,
Like the fair light of dawn, or summer eve
On rippling stream, or cloud-reflecting lake.
And looking to the heaven, that bends above you,
How oft! I bless the lot that made me love you.

Thomas Carew

(1595-1640)

Ingrateful Beauty Threatened

Know Celia, since thou art so proud
'Twas I that gave thee thy renown;
Thou hadst, in the forgotten crowd
Of common beauties, lived unknown,
Had not my verse exhaled thy name,
And with it imp'd the wings of fame.

That killing power is none of thine,
I gave it to thy voice, and eyes;
Thy sweets, thy graces, all are mine;
Thou art my star, shin'st in my skies;
Then dart not from thy borrowed sphere
Lightning on him that fixed thee there.

Tempt me with such affrights no more,
Lest what I made, I uncreate;
Let fools thy mystic forms adore,
I'll know thee in thy mortal state;
Wise poets that wrapped truth in tales,
Knew her themselves, through all her veils.

Thomas Carew
(1595-1640)

To My Inconstant Mistress

When thou, poor excommunicate
From all the joys of love, shalt see
The full reward, and glorious fate,
Which my strong faith shall purchase me,
Then curse thine own inconstancy.

A fairer hand than thine, shall cure
That heart, which thy false oaths did wound;
And to my soul, a soul more pure
Than thine, shall by love's hand be bound
And both with equal glory crowned.

Then shalt thou weep, entreat, complain
To Llve, as I did once to thee;
When all thy tears shall be as vain
As mine were then, for thou shalt be
Dammed for thy false apostasy.

Thomas Carew
(1595-1640)

Mediocrity In Love Rejected

Give me more love or more disdain;
The torrid, or the frozen zone,
Bring equal ease unto my pain;
The temperate affords me none;
Either extreme, of love, or hate,
Is sweeter than a calm estate.

Give me a storm; if it be love,
Like Danae in that golden shower
I swim in pleasure; if it prove
Disdain, that torrent will devour
My vulture-hopes; and he's possessed
Of heaven, that's but from hell released:

Then crown my joys, or cure my pain;
Give me more love, or more disdain.

Thomas Hardy
(1840-1928)

A Broken Appointment

You did not come,
And marching time drew on, and wore me numb,—
Yet less for loss of your dear presence there
Than that I thus found lacking in your make
That high compassion which can overbear
Reluctance for pure loving kindness' sake
Grieved I, when, as the hope-hour stroked its sum,
You did not come.

You love not me,
And love alone can lend you loyalty;
—I know and knew it. But, unto the store
Of human deeds divine in all but name,
Was it not worth a little hour or more
To add yet this: Once you, a woman, came
To soothe a time-torn man; even though it be
You love not me?

Thomas Moore
(1779-1852)

Oh, Call It By Some Better Name

Oh, call it by some better name,
For friendship sounds too cold,
While love is now a worldly flame,
Whose shrine must be of gold:
And passion, like the sun at noon,
That burns o'er all he sees,
Awhile as warm will set as soon—
Then call it none of these.

Imagine something purer far,
More free from stain of clay
Than friendship, love, or passion are,
Yet human, still as they:
And if thy lip, for love like this,
No mortal word can frame,
Go, ask of angels what it is,
And call it by that name!

Thomas Moore
(1779-1852)

The Time I've Lost In Wooing

The time I've lost in wooing,
In watching and pursuing
The light, that lies
In woman's eyes,
Has been my heart's undoing.
Though wisdom oft has sought me,
I scorned the lore she brought me,
My only books
Were woman's looks,
And folly's all they've taught me.

Her smile when beauty granted,
I hung with gaze enchanted,
Like him the sprite,
Whom maids by night
Oft meet in glen that's haunted.
Like him, too, beauty won me,
But while her eyes were on me,
If once their ray
Was turned away,
Oh! winds could not outrun me.

And are those follies going?
And is my proud heart growing
Too cold or wise
For brilliant eyes
Again to set it glowing?

Thomas Moore
(1779-1852)

[...]

No, vain, alas! the endeavour
From bonds so sweet to sever;
Poor wisdom's chance
Against a glance
Is now as weak as ever.

Thomas Moore
(1779-1852)

My Heart and Lute

I give thee all — I can no more —
Though poor the offering be;
My heart and lute are all the store
That I can bring to thee.
A lute whose gentle song reveals
The soul of love full well;
And, better far, a heart that feels
Much more than lute could tell.

Though love and song may fail, alas!
To keep life's clouds away,
At least 't will make them lighter pass,
Or gild them if they stay.
And even if care at moments flings
A discord o'er life's happy strain,
Let love but gently touch the strings,
'T will all be sweet again!

Sir Thomas Wyatt
(1503-1542)

They Flee From Me

They flee from me that sometime did me seek
With naked foot, stalking in my chamber.
I have seen them gentle, tame, and meek,
That now are wild and do not remember
That sometime they put themself in danger
To take bread at my hand; and now they range,
Busily seeking with a continual change.

Thanked be fortune it hath been otherwise
Twenty times better; but once in special,
In thin array after a pleasant guise,
When her loose gown from her shoulders did fall,
And she me caught in her arms long and small;
Therewithall sweetly did me kiss
And softly said, "Dear heart, how like you this?"

It was no dream: I lay broad waking.
But all is turned thorough my gentleness
Into a strange fashion of forsaking;
And I have leave to go of her goodness,
And she also, to use newfangleness.
But since that I so kindly am served
I would fain know what she hath deserved.

Sir Thomas Wyatt
(1503-1542)

Whoso List To Hunt

Whoso list to hunt, I know where is an hind,
But as for me, alas, I may no more.
The vain travail hath wearied me so sore,
I am of them that farthest cometh behind.
Yet may I by no means my wearied mind
Draw from the deer, but as she fleeth afore
Fainting I follow. I leave off therefore,
Since in a net I seek to hold the wind.
Who list her hunt, I put him out of doubt,
As well as I may spend his time in vain.
And graven with diamonds in letters plain
There is written, her fair neck round about:
"*Noli me tangere*, for Caesar's I am,
And wild for to hold, though I seem tame."

Sir Thomas Wyatt
(1503-1542)

Farewell love

Farewell love and all thy laws for ever;
Thy baited hooks shall tangle me no more.
Senec and Plato call me from thy lore
To perfect wealth, my wit for to endeavour.
In blind error when I did persever,
Thy sharp repulse, that pricketh aye so sore,
Hath taught me to set in trifles no store
And scape forth, since liberty is lever.
Therefore farewell; go trouble younger hearts
And in me claim no more authority.
With idle youth go use thy property
And thereon spend thy many brittle darts,
For hitherto though I have lost all my time,
Me lusteth no longer rotten boughs to climb.

Walt Whitman
(1819-1892)

A Glimpse

A glimpse through an interstice caught,
Of a crowd of workmen and drivers in a bar-room
    around the stove late of a winter night, and I
    unremarked seated in a corner,
Of a youth who loves me and whom I love, silently
    approaching and seating himself near, that he may
    hold me by the hand,
A long while amid the noises of coming and going, of
    drinking and oath and smutty jest,
There we two, content, happy in being together,
    speaking little, perhaps not a word.

Walt Whitman
(1819-1892)

To a Stranger

Passing stranger! you do not know
How longingly I look upon you,
You must be he I was seeking,
Or she I was seeking
(It comes to me as a dream)

I have somewhere surely
Lived a life of joy with you,
All is recalled as we flit by each other,
Fluid, affectionate, chaste, matured,

You grew up with me,
Were a boy with me or a girl with me,
I ate with you and slept with you,
your body has become
not yours only nor left my body mine only,

You give me the pleasure of your eyes,
face, flesh as we pass,
You take of my beard, breast, hands,
in return,

I am not to speak to you, I am to think of you
when I sit alone or wake at night, alone
I am to wait, I do not doubt I am to meet you again
I am to see to it that I do not lose you.

Sir Walter Raleigh
(1552-1618)

The Silent Lover

I
Passions are likened best to floods and streams:
The shallow murmur, but the deep are dumb;
So, when affections yield discourse, it seems
The bottom is but shallow whence they come.
They that are rich in words, in words discover
That they are poor in that which makes a lover.

II
Wrong not, sweet empress of my heart,
The merit of true passion,
With thinking that he feels no smart,
That sues for no compassion;

Since, if my plaints serve not to approve
The conquest of thy beauty,
It comes not from defect of love,
But from excess of duty.

For, knowing that I sue to serve
A saint of such perfection,
As all desire, but none deserve,
A place in her affection,

I rather choose to want relief
Than venture the revealing;
Where glory recommends the grief,
Despair distrusts the healing.

Sir Walter Raleigh
(1552-1618)

[...]

Thus those desires that aim too high
For any mortal lover,
When reason cannot make them die,
Discretion doth them cover.

Yet, when discretion doth bereave
The plaints that they should utter,
Then thy discretion may perceive
That silence is a suitor.

Silence in love bewrays more woe
Than words, though ne'er so witty:
A beggar that is dumb, you know,
May challenge double pity.

Then wrong not, dearest to my heart,
My true, though secret, passion:
He smarteth most that hides his smart,
And sues for no compassion.

Sir Walter Raleigh
(1552-1618)

A farewell to False Love

Farewell, false love, the oracle of lies,
A mortal foe and enemy to rest,
An envious boy, from whom all cares arise,
A bastard vile, a beast with rage possessed,
A way of error, a temple full of treason,
In all effects contrary unto reason.

A poisoned serpent covered all with flowers,
Mother of sighs, and murderer of repose,
A sea of sorrows whence are drawn such showers
As moisture lend to every grief that grows;
A school of guile, a net of deep deceit,
A gilded hook that holds a poisoned bait.

A fortress foiled, which reason did defend,
A siren song, a fever of the mind,
A maze wherein affection finds no end,
A raging cloud that runs before the wind,
A substance like the shadow of the sun,
A goal of grief for which the wisest run.

A quenchless fire, a nurse of trembling fear,
A path that leads to peril and mishap,
A true retreat of sorrow and despair,
An idle boy that sleeps in pleasure's lap,
A deep mistrust of that which certain seems,
A hope of that which reason doubtful deems.

Sir Walter Raleigh
(1552-1618)

[...]

Sith then thy trains my younger years betrayed,
And for my faith ingratitude I find;
And sith repentance hath my wrongs bewrayed,
Whose course was ever contrary to kind:
False love, desire, and beauty frail, adieu!
Dead is the root whence all these fancies grew.

William Blake

(1757-1827)

My Pretty Rose Tree

A flower was offered to me,
Such a flower as May never bore;
But I said, "I've a pretty rose tree,"
And I passed the sweet flower o'er.

Then I went to my pretty rose tree,
To tend her by day and by night;
But my rose turned away with jealousy,
And her thorns were my only delight.

William Blake
(1757-1827)

The Garden of Love

I went to the Garden of Love,
And saw what I never had seen;
A Chapel was built in the midst,
Where I used to play on the green.

And the gates of this Chapel were shut,
And "Thou shalt not" writ over the door;
So I turned to the Garden of Love
That so many sweet flowers bore.

And I saw it was filled with graves,
And tombstones where flowers should be;
And Priests in black gowns were walking their
    rounds,
And binding with briars my joys & desires.

William Blake
(1757-1827)

Love's Secret

Never seek to tell thy love,
Love that never told can be;
For the gentle wind does move
Silently, invisibly.

I told my love, I told my love,
I told her all my heart;
Trembling, cold, in ghastly fears,
Ah! she did depart!

Soon as she was gone from me,
A traveler came by,
Silently, invisibly
He took her with a sigh.

William Cowper
(1731-1800)

To A Young Lady

Sweet stream that winds through yonder glade,
Apt emblem of a virtuous maid
Silent and chaste she steals along,
Far from the world's gay busy throng:
With gentle yet prevailing force,
Intent upon her destined course;
Graceful and useful all she does,
Blessing and blest where'er she goes;
Pure-bosomed as that watery glass,
And Heaven reflected in her face.

William Morris
(1834-1896)

Love Is Enough

Love is enough: though the world be a-waning,
And the woods have no voice but the voice of
  complaining,
Though the skies be too dark for dim eyes to
  discover
The gold-cups and daisies fair blooming
  thereunder.
Though the hills be held shadows, and the sea a
  dark wonder,
And this day draw a veil over all deeds passed over,
Yet their hands shall not tremble, their feet shall
  not falter:
The void shall not weary, the fear shall not alter
These lips and these eyes of the loved and the lover.

William Shakespeare
(1564-1616)

Sonnet XVIII

Shall I compare thee to a summer's day?
Thou art more lovely and more temperate.
Rough winds do shake the darling buds of May,
And summer's lease hath all too short a date.
Sometime too hot the eye of heaven shines,
And often is his gold complexion dimmed;
And every fair from fair sometime declines,
By chance, or nature's changing course,
    untrimmed;
But thy eternal summer shall not fade,
Nor lose possession of that fair thou owest,
Nor shall death brag thou wanderest in his shade,
When in eternal lines to time thou growest.
So long as men can breathe, or eyes can see,
So long lives this, and this gives life to thee.

William Shakespeare
(1564-1616)

Sonnet XL

Take all my loves, my love, yea, take them all:
What hast thou then more than thou hadst before?
No love, my love, that thou mayst true love call—
All mine was thine before thou hadst this more.
Then if for my love thou my love receivest,
I cannot blame thee for my love thou usest;
But yet be blamed if thou this self deceivest
By wilful taste of what thyself refusest.
I do forgive thy robbery, gentle thief,
Although thou steal thee all my poverty;
And yet love knows it is a greater grief
To bear love's wrong than hate's known injury.
   Lascivious grace, in whom all ill well shows,
   Kill me with spites, yet we must not be foes.

William Shakespeare
(1564-1616)

Sonnet CXVI

Let me not to the marriage of true minds
Admit impediments. Love is not love
Which alters when it alteration finds,
Or bends with the remover to remove:
O no! it is an ever-fixed mark
That looks on tempests and is never shaken;
It is the star to every wandering bark,
Whose worth's unknown, although his height be
  taken.
Love's not time's fool, though rosy lips and
  cheeks
Within his bending sickle's compass come:
Love alters not with his brief hours and weeks,
But bears it out even to the edge of doom.
If this be error and upon me proved,
I never writ, nor no man ever loved.

William Shakespeare
(1564-1616)

Sonnet CXLVII

My love is as a fever, longing still
For that which longer nurseth the disease,
Feeding on that which doth preserve the ill,
The uncertain sickly appetite to please.
My reason, the physician to my love,
Angry that his prescriptions are not kept,
Hath left me, and I desperate now approve
Desire is death, which physic did except.
Past cure I am, now reason is past care,
And frantic-mad with evermore unrest;
My thoughts and my discourse as madmen's are,
At random from the truth vainly expressed;
For I have sworn thee fair and thought thee bright,
Who art as black as hell, as dark as night.

William Shakespeare
(1564-1616)

Antony & Cleopatra, Act II, Scene II

The barge she sat in, like a burnished throne,
Burned on the water: the poop was beaten gold;
Purple the sails, and so perfumed that
The winds were lovesick with them; the oars were
   silver,
Which to the tune of flutes kept stroke, and made
The water which they beat to follow faster,
As amorous of their strokes. For her own person,
It beggared all description: she did lie
In her pavilion, cloth-of-gold of tissue,
O'erpicturing that Venus where we see
The fancy outwork nature: on each side her
Stood pretty dimpled boys, like smiling Cupids,
With divers-coloured fans, whose wind did seem
To glow the delicate cheeks which they did cool,
And what they undid did.

William Wordsworth

(1770-1850)

Louisa

I met Louisa in the shade,
And, having seen that lovely maid,
Why should I fear to say
That, nymph-like, she is fleet and strong,
And down the rocks can leap along
Like rivulets in May?

She loves her fire, her cottage-home;
Yet o'er the moorland will she roam
In weather rough and bleak;
And, when against the wind she strains,
Oh! might I kiss the mountain rains
That sparkle on her cheek.

Take all that's mine "beneath the moon",
If I with her but half a noon
May sit beneath the walls
Of some old cave, or mossy nook,
When up she winds along the brook
To hunt the waterfalls.

William Wordsworth
(1770-1850)

She Dwelt Among the Untrodden Ways

She dwelt among the untrodden ways
Beside the springs of Dove,
A Maid whom there were none to praise
And very few to love:

A violet by a mossy stone
Half hidden from the eye!
—Fair as a star, when only one
Is shining in the sky.

She lived unknown, and few could know
When Lucy ceased to be;
But she is in her grave, and, oh,
The difference to me!

William Wordsworth
(1770-1850)

Perfect Woman

She was a phantom of delight
When first she gleamed upon my sight;
A lovely apparition, sent
To be a moment's ornament;
Her eyes as stars of twilight fair;
Like twilight's, too, her dusky hair;
But all things else about her drawn
From May-time and the cheerful dawn;
A dancing shape, an image gay,
To haunt, to startle, and waylay.

I saw her upon nearer view,
A Spirit, yet a Woman too!
Her household motions light and free,
And steps of virgin liberty;
A countenance in which did meet
Sweet records, promises as sweet;
A creature not too bright or good
For human nature's daily food,
For transient sorrows, simple wiles,
Praise, blame, love, kisses, tears, and smiles.

And now I see with eye serene
The very pulse of the machine;
A being breathing thoughtful breath,
A traveller between life and death;
The reason firm, the temperate will,

William Wordsworth
(1770-1850)

[...]

Endurance, foresight, strength, and skill;
A perfect Woman, nobly planned,
To warn, to comfort, and command;
And yet a Spirit still, and bright
With something of angelic light.

William Butler Yeats
(1865-1939)

The Ragged Wood

O hurry where by water among the trees
The delicate-stepping stag and his lady sigh,
When they have but looked upon their images—
Would none had ever loved but you and I!

Or have you heard that sliding silver-shoed
Pale silver-proud queen-woman of the sky,
When the sun looked out of his golden hood?—
O that none ever loved but you and I!

O hurry to the ragged wood, for there
I will drive all those lovers out and cry—
O my share of the world, O yellow hair!
No one has ever loved but you and I.

William Butler Yeats
(1865-1939)

A Drinking Song

Wine comes in at the mouth
And love comes in at the eye;
That's all we shall know for truth
Before we grow old and die.
I lift the glass to my mouth,
I look at you, and I sigh.

William Butler Yeats
(1865-1939)

Never give all the heart

Never give all the heart, for love
Will hardly seem worth thinking of
To passionate women if it seem
Certain, and they never dream
That it fades out from kiss to kiss;
For everything that's lovely is
But a brief, dreamy, kind delight.
O never give the heart outright,
For they, for all smooth lips can say,
Have given their hearts up to the play.
And who could play it well enough
If deaf and dumb and blind with love?
He that made this knows all the cost,
For he gave all his heart and lost.

INDEX OF FIRST LINES   **Page:**

INDEX OF FIRST LINES   **Page:**

INDEX OF FIRST LINES   **Page:**

INDEX OF FIRST LINES   Page:

INDEX OF FIRST LINES   **Page:**